Series / Number 03-014

Environmental Policies in Canada, Sweden, and the United States: A Comparative Overview

LENNART J. LUNDQVIST
Uppsala University, Sweden

SAGE PUBLICATIONS / Beverly Hills / London

For information address:

SAGE PUBLICATIONS, INC.
275 South Beverly Drive
Beverly Hills, California 90212

SAGE PUBLICATIONS LTD
St George's House / 44 Hatton Garden
London EC1N 8ER

International Standard Book Number 0-8039-0368-5

Library of Congress Catalog Card No. 73-92225

FIRST PRINTING

When citing a professional paper, please use the proper form. Remember to cite the
correct Sage Professional Paper series title and include the paper number. One of the
two following formats can be adapted (depending on the style manual used):

(1) OSTROM, E. et al. (1973) "Community Organization and the Provision of Police
Services." Sage Professional Papers in Administrative and Policy Studies, 1, 03-001.
Beverly Hills and London: Sage Pubns.

OR

(2) Ostrom, Elinor, et al. 1973. *Community Organization and the Provision of Police
Services.* Sage Professional Papers in Administrative and Policy Studies, vol. 1, series
no. 03-001. Beverly Hills and London: Sage Publications.

CONTENTS

Problems and Issues in Comparative Environmental Policy Analysis 5

From Fragments to Policy: "Environment" Becomes the Focus 8

From Input to Output: The Making of Environmental Policies 13

Within the Output: Area and Content of Environmental Policies 21

From Output to Outcome: Implementation and Enforcement of
    Air Quality Programs 29

All the Way Around—Environmental Policies and Change 35

Concluding Remarks 38

References 39

Environmental Policies in Canada, Sweden, and the United States: A Comparative Overview

LENNART J. LUNDQVIST
Uppsala University, Sweden

PROBLEMS AND ISSUES IN COMPARATIVE ENVIRONMENTAL POLICY ANALYSIS

At present, comparative policy analysis seems to possess at least four characteristics. First, comparative policy studies at a cross-national level are as yet uncommon; most work has been done on a cross-regional level. Second, there is as yet no agreement on terminology; even such important concepts as policy-making, policy content, and policy impact lack commonly accepted definitions. Third, a wide range of approaches are considered appropriate for comparative policy studies; most scholars take an eclectic view as to models and methods (Rose, 1972 and 1973a; Sharkansky, 1970). Fourth, underlying most of what is being done in the field of policy analysis is the preoccupancy with the "relevance" of such studies to the actual policy process: what factors promote or prohibit desired changes (Lundqvist, 1973a)?

These characteristics of comparative policy analysis are also part of the problems and issues that emerge in the comparative study of environmental policy. Such studies are still mostly in the planning stage. With

AUTHOR'S NOTE: *Part of a larger study of environmental policy and political change, the research for this paper has been supported by the American-Scandinavian Foundation; the National Science Foundation; the Swedish Social Science Research Council; and the Helge Ax:son Johnson Foundation. I am especially grateful to Professor Lynton K. Caldwell at Indiana University for intellectual advice and support; and to Maude for the kind of support that only a wife can give.*

respect to terminology, the very term "environmental" suggests the difficulties of defining the subject of analysis. The concept of "environment" may have different connotations in different countries. And the subject becomes more elusive over time, as "environmental" concerns penetrate more and more areas of governmental activity. The broad scope of this policy field suggests that no single model or method will be adequate to describe and explain its character and development. The size of environmental problems and the amount of political change needed to cope with them seem to make "relevance" a necessity.

On the other hand, environmental policies possess certain characteristics which seem to outweigh many of the difficulties inherent in comparative policy research. I think here of the almost simultaneous, and many times dramatic, emergence of the environmental problem on the political agenda. Within eight years, from 1965 to 1973, the problem of "environmental quality" developed into an issue of public concern in most industrialized countries. In this short span of time, it has produced an increasing number and variety of policies, programs, organizational changes and other activities. Although having many similarities with regard to socio-economic conditions, the industrialized countries show considerable variations in their structures, cultures, and ideologies. All these conditions contribute to environmental policy's very rich potential for comparative policy analysis.

To fully utilize this potential, however, the scholar must first of all engage in a careful definition of his subject. Numerous definitions exist, none of which seem easy to operationalize. If used, they would lead the scholar to include "practically everything" in his analysis. The difficulties of such a formidable task make it necessary to look for other alternatives (always, of course, aware of the risks inherent in oversimplification or reductionism). This study attempts the following definition: "Environmental policy is governmental action taken to solve the problems of the society's relationship to its physical environment." The concept of "physical environment" includes the elements of air, water, and soil with their ingredients, organisms, and features. For the purpose of this study, the inner parts of such man-made surroundings as houses, factories, etc. are excluded, although the boundaries are hard to draw in certain cases, such as environmental health and safety factors in mines, factories, and places of public assembly. "Environmental problems" refer to results of human and societal actions which are perceived as undesired or harmful to the physical environment. Although this definition is not exhaustive or unproblematic, it is hoped that it will enable the student to identify those phenomena in the real world that constitute the substance of environmental policies in most countries.

To further utilize this potential, Canada, Sweden, and the United States are chosen as the countries for comparison. It is hoped that the considerable structural and cultural differences among these countries will lead to interesting results regarding the features of their environmental policies. There is, however, need for a framework that increases the possibilities of comparison and of generalization of the findings. The main concepts in this framework are *political change* and *policy*. The content of political change has at least four dimensions: (1) the character and distribution of values, (2) the control of governments, (3) the institutional structure, and (4) the behavior of the actors in the political system. As a process, political change can be studied in the following dimensions: (1) an "initial" state, (2) a period of changes in the environment implying new conditions for political activity and for the political system, (3) activities by political elites to produce new policies and coalitions, (4) a period of policy implementation implying changes in the political system and in its environment. A fifth stage, in the form of a "consequent" or "resulting" state, may also be discernible.

Central in the process of political change is policy, which is seen both as a dependent and an independent varible. The content of policy has at least three components: (1) statements of intents or goals to be achieved, (2) recommendations concerning the ways and means of implementation, and (3) the actual performance levels of those implementing the policy. As a process, policy ranges all the way from initiation to the stages of evaluation and feedback.

To increase the general comparativeness of this framework, certain factors have been identified as potentially influential on policy processes and contents:

(1) ideologies, values, and structures of political systems;

(2) historical development, habit and routine in policy-making;

(3) power relations among groups affected by environmental problems and policies;

(4) considerations of utility; and

(5) existence and use of issue-relevant knowledge in the policy field [Lundqvist, 1973b].

Given the vast size and complexity of the environmental policy field and the amount of activity of different levels of government over the last years, it is obvious that a study like this one—done by one scholar alone—cannot pretend to give *the* picture of environmental policies in the three countries. Such an enterprise will need the combined efforts of many scholars from many disciplines. My study is thus confined to some main features of national environmental policies in these countries. It is hoped that with these qualifications in mind, the reader will look at the results of the study—however preliminary and tentative they may be—as an input to the discussion of "what questions should be asked" in future comparative policy studies.

FROM FRAGMENTS TO POLICY

"ENVIRONMENT" BECOMES THE FOCUS

It would be more than foolish to suggest that environmental problems had not been politically observed or tackled before the mid-1960s. But although there were several programs, they remained fragmented and inconsistent. While most governments of industrialized countries became increasingly occupied with comprehensive policies of public health, social welfare, and economic growth, there seemed to be a paradoxical neglect of the ultimate dependence on a quantitatively and qualitatively sound physical environment for the achievement of the goals of these policies. At the same time, new technologies and methods of achieving these socio-economic policy goals increasingly depreciated the physical environment.

What happened in the 1960s could be characterized as the convergence of events and factors to the "agendization" of environmental problems in a more comprehensive fashion. This process seems to have been an interplay of objective and subjective factors. Objectively, the demands on natural resources for the achievement of socio-economic goals, and the immense environmental side-effects of new technologies to satisfy resource demands made the societies' relationships to the physical environment more and more problematic. At the same time, science and technology were beginning to develop tools and methods whereby a much more comprehensive and objective assessment of the environmental effects of economic and social activities could be carried out. The very success of industrial societies in achieving socio-economic goals increased the number of welfare state members whose cultural and consumption patterns indicated that they formed an important potential basis for environmental policy demands. Subjectively, many depreciative factors in the environment seemed to reach a "critical mass," and triggered off an increase in individual perception of environmental problems.

Given the existence of many similarities in socio-economic and technological conditions of the countries studied here, it is not surprising to find several similarities in the process of environmental "agendization." On the other hand, there are differences which seem to reflect the interplay of objective and subjective factors just mentioned. "Agendization" is not just a result of public perception of a problem and public demand for political action to solve it.

Unfortunately for comparative efforts, opinion polls on the environmental issue have been taken regularly only in the United States, and the phrasing of questions differs considerably between countries. There is, however, substantial evidence that environmental opinion has increased rather conspicuously over the last years. Between 1965 and 1969, the percentage of the United States population viewing pollution as serious increased from 28 to 69 for air pollution and from 35 to 74 for water pollution. With regard to demands for political action, the percentage that would like to see more devotion from politicians to pollution problems rose from 17 in 1965 to 41 in 1971. While 50 percent of the 1967 poll wanted more federal money for environmental programs, this was demanded by 83 percent in 1971. And while a minority of 44 percent in the 1967 poll said it was willing to pay $15 extra in federal taxes to fight air pollution, this had grown to a majority of 59 percent in 1971 (Erskine, 1972).

Three opinion polls were held in Sweden in 1969 concerning the environmental problem. They revealed that 84 percent of the Swedes were in favor of putting special charges on polluting industries. A majority of 69 percent was amenable to higher local taxes to fight water pollution, while 54 percent found it "desirable" to cut down the growth rate of the GNP in order to save the environment from deterioration (Lundqvist, 1972a: 92 f.). An early 1970 Canadian poll showed that 69 percent of the population considered the dangers of pollution very serious. Later in that year, another poll found that reducing pollution of air and water was named *the* top domestic problem by 65 percent, which was more than for any other domestic problem mentioned (Canadian Institute of Public Opinion, 1970a and 1970b). In all three countries, this increase in public opinion coincided with an increase in mass media's coverage of environmental issues. In the United States, the media increased their coverage by over 300 percent in a few years, and the content shifted from traditional conservation problems to broader environmental problems connected with industrialization and urbanization (McEvoy III, 1972). In Sweden, the number of newspaper editorials on environmental problems was six times larger in 1968 than it had been in 1963 (Lundqvist, 1971: 106). It seems safe to assume the same trend prevailed in Canada, perhaps starting a few years later.

[10]

Two other factors seem to have operated in the rise of public awareness in all three countries. A series of events, such as oil spills, DDT, mercury, and phosphate "crises" occurred and undoubtedly aroused public apprehension. Likewise, there was everywhere an emergence of a new breed of environmental scientists, who never hesitated to take their findings to the public and to help organize environmental pressure groups to activate the policy-makers. May it suffice here to mention such examples as "Pollution Probe" in Canada, the "Earth Day" movement in the United States, and the "byalag" movement in Sweden. Overall, the environmental issue has resulted in the formation of new groups and coalitions cutting across established political cleavages. At the same time, it has grown to a political force that cannot be neglected by politicians, since all opinion polls give evidence that the movement is dominated by upper middle class strata and educated youth groups.

With all these similarities in public perception of environmental problems and demands for political action, it would be tempting to conclude that the "agendization" of environmental problems has proceeded in much the same way in all three countries. But a closer look reveals that this process is more than governmental response to growing demands. Governments can be ahead of demands, be it through careful study and assessment of prevailing objective conditions and their future development, or through skillful imagination and assessment of future trends in public opinion.

The Swedish pattern seems to have been one of anticipation of future public demands. In the early 1960s, several Royal Commissions (the classical way of formulating Swedish policies) were set up, or were already working. In 1963, the Government announced that it planned to formulate an overall "environmental" policy when more of the Commission Reports were delivered or nearly finished. And with the convergence of several Reports and findings of these Commissions, the Government introduced an Environmental Policy Bill in 1965, well before the upsurge in environmental opinion. From that year, the parties increased their activities considerably, both by adopting "environmental" platforms and by sponsoring "environmental" bills in the Parliament (Lundqvist, 1971: 105 and 110 f.).

The remarkable thing about this anticipatory behavior is that it occurred in a country relatively less affected by environmental disruption than many other countries. Structural factors probably played a large part. The close structural links between the governing Social Democratic Party and the Trade Unions helped attract the Cabinet's attention to the problems of increasing demands for outdoor recreation, and made it

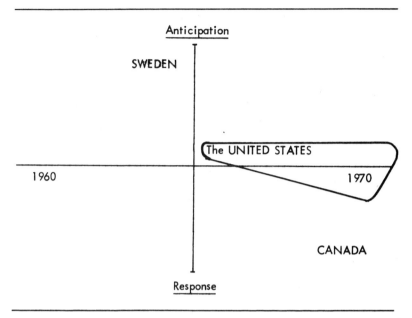

Figure 1: Patterns of "Agendization" of the "Environmental" Issue in Canada, Sweden, and the United States: Timing and Type of Political Action.

sensitive to environmental problems. And the unique Swedish combination of structural cooperation and cultural "compromise-mindedness" made it easy to accommodate the environmental concern into an already relatively thoroughly planned economy, and to obtain the acceptance of the industrial interests. The "agendization" was thus a matter at the top political and organizational level, without the legitimacy of the new policy area being seriously questioned.

The process is much more complicated in the United States balance-of-powers system. As in Sweden, several programs pertinent to the environment had been established before the mid-1960s, but also as in Sweden, they lacked coherence. The year 1965 seems to indicate a new turn, with President Johnson launching his policy of "Natural Beauty," and with bills introduced in the Congress, calling for a national "environmental" policy. In the following years, an increased activity could be seen in Congress, and in 1969, the Congress passed the now famous National Environmental Policy Act, which established the principles of a United States environmental policy (Caldwell, 1971: 174-180). But around 1970, there was also the tremendous increase in public demand, which caused a "join-the-bandwagon" effect among policy-makers. "Everybody" in the Congress and in the Administration rushed to respond in order to get credit in the new field (Jones, 1972).

What is remarkable about the United States development is the combination of anticipation and response, and the more dramatic turn in political action. It is generally held that the "Natural Beauty" policy was ahead of public opinion, as was probably the comprehensive "environmental" prespective taken by some Congressmen working on the formulation of a national environmental policy. But as the 1960s went on, the increase in public demand was bound to affect the behavior of the legislators in the "personality"-geared American system. The passage of the NEPA was a surprisingly smooth affair, and did not in any sense imply the dramatic turn of events in 1970.

There are several structural and cultural factors that could explain the American experience. Unlike a Prime Minister in a parliamentary system, the American President cannot set the agenda and expect it to be realized through swift legislative action. On the other hand he has certain possibilities for keeping a problem area in the "non-policy" range. Thus Richard Nixon was objecting to the National Environmental Policy Act during most of 1969. But when he realized how important environmental opinion had become in American politics, he tried to exploit it as a political resource. This can be seen in his symbolic gesture of choosing NEPA as the first act to sign into law in the 1970s. The environmental issue could not be channeled through a coherent party system, but on the other hand, it could capitalize upon the responsiveness fostered by personality politics. But many politicians were committed to the idea of unfettered economic growth, and linked to strong industrial interests. Since the American environmentalists had no strong consumer-oriented interest organizations to which they could turn, they probably had no alternative but to form new groups and demand political response through dramatic action. In addition, many problems in the American environment seem more severe than those elsewhere.

The Canadian process is typically one of response to increasing public demands. Not until after the 1968 election did Canadian politicians take up the "environmental" issue. Then it was announced by the Cabinet in the Speech of the Throne, but it was not until the fall of 1969 that any action took place. Then there was a considerable activity among the politicians with a number of Cabinet and Private Member's Bills (Dwivedi, 1972-1973).

Several reasons can be given for this late Canadian reaction. With regard to structure, the Canadian Prime Minister is hindered in his agenda-setting activity by the Constitution. In the case of the environment, no national policy can be launched until the constitutionality and the jurisdictional matters have been clarified, and an agreement reached between the Prime Minister and his "peers," the Prime Ministers of the Provinces, since the jurisdiction is a shared one. Also "spatial-environmental" factors seem to have been at work. The recognition of the seriousness of the environmental situation was hampered by the Canadians' belief in the vastness and richness of their resources relative to the population. It was not until groups such as Pollution Probe entered the scene that this belief began to wither away. On the other hand, this factor became part of the cultural change in the late 1970s with the emergence of a Canadian nationalism. When the Americans started proposing exports of Canadian resources to supply the needs of America, this was denounced by the nationalists and no doubt formed part of the upsurge in public environmental demand, thus influencing the response around 1970.

Despite the similarities in the environmental opinion of the three countries, and despite similarities in socio-economic and technological development, we thus find that the process of putting the environmental issue on the political agenda has been different in all three countries. Political and power structures, cultural values, and—in the Canadian case—"spatial" considerations all seem to have had an impact on these differences in timing and type of political action.

FROM INPUT TO OUTPUT

THE MAKING OF ENVIRONMENTAL POLICIES

One of the ideas surrounding the environmental issue has been its allegedly unique character. It has been said to represent something qualitatively "new" in politics, not easily lending itself to the existing methods of compromise and satisficing strategies in group politics. But rather than looking for differences relative to other policy areas, one should look for the principal characteristics of environmental policies. Four such characteristics have been suggested:

(1) scientific and technical complexity—thus creating major knowledge needs for policy-makers;

(2) association with affluence and achievement;

(3) costly and far-reaching effects; and

(4) different priority among different social groups [Jones, 1972].

If these are general characteristics, they should become visible in a comparative analysis of how environmental policies are formulated and legitimized. One would also expect to find some relation between the way in which the issue is brought to the agenda, the need for knowledge, and the "style" of policy-making. By the last term I refer to a wide range of alternatives, from disjointed incrementalism to spectacular escalation or augmentation. One would also expect to find out whether or not the traditional way of making policies is more dominant than changes called for by the characteristics of environmental problems.

The general style of Swedish policy-making is said to be incremental; it is deliberative, rationalistic, open and consensual (Anton, 1969). Once the Cabinet sees an issue as "political," it gives it constantly increasing attention and very great efforts are made to assert the political and technical feasibility of the proposed action. Affected interests usually work almost as parts of the governmental system during the policy formulation, and decisions on policy are worked out—or allowed to "mature"—in an atmosphere of consensus. It is thus a steady, ongoing process rather than ad hoc response (Hancock, 1972: 202 ff.). One would expect then that this way of making policy would fit in very well with the characteristics of environmental policies. And a brief review of the national policy development suggests that this is the case. Legislation and policy programs have proceeded incrementally toward the building of a national system of environmental control, based on cooperation and consultation between politicians, administrators, and affected interests. Three stages can be identified:

pre- 1965: investigation and problem definition;
1965-1969: establishment of a national environmental policy and specific action programs; and
1970-   : constant review of ongoing programs, and incremental changes in policy.

Already mentioned is the number of Royal Commissions working in the 1960s. Represented in these Commissions were the political parties, the major interest organizations, the bureaucratic expertise, and to some extent scientific experts. The function of these Commissions was to investigate and define the problem, to recommend action, and to assert that this action would be politically and technically possible, generally through compromises. Mostly, affected interests were—at least in principle—amenable to the compromises reached in the Commissions. And although the announcement of the Environmental Policy in 1965 meant an escalation in policy activity, this never went beyond the drive for an appropriate increase in knowledge as a basis for action. The feasibility of the goals was thus further investigated in three respects: administrative integration and manpower resources, environmental research, and legislation. Throughout all the stages, there has thus been a drive for political and technological feasibility, which is to some extent surprising in view of the mostly very vague goals of the policy. Since 1968-1969, there has been an expansion of the number of participants in policy development, a more active competition among the politicians, and a constant monitoring of policy development by the media. This has created a group of "ecologists" among the politicians who want to see the prevailing incrementalism substituted by a policy escalation, aimed at maximizing ecological goals. But even this group stresses the need for adequate knowledge preceding action. Another sign of change is the increasing role of the environmental bureaucracy in policy formulation, as can be seen in the number of Parliamentary Committee reports accepting without question the commentaries given by administrators. But this sign does not deny the characteristics of environmental policy, i.e., its dependence on and basis in scientific knowledge, nor is it in any way incompatible with the incrementalist style (Lundqvist, 1973c).

Canadian policy-making shares at least two commonalities with the Swedish style: incrementalism, and Cabinet and bureaucracy dominance. But as mentioned above, the constraints posed by the constitutional ambiguities over environmental jurisdiction heavily affect the Cabinet's position. It has restrained Ottawa from explicitly coming out in favor of nation-wide policy goals. At the same time, the evidently national character of the problems has made a nationwide effort necessary. This has resulted in some very specific sets of consultation and cooperation in Canadian environmental policy-making, thus making the typical Canadian federal-provincial "negotiations" form part of this policy process (Simeon, 1971; Doern and Aucoin, 1971). And despite the considerable escalation in policy over the last few years, these constraints have proved strong enough to make the incremental policy-making prevail. The following stages can be (tentatively) defined:

1969-1971: escalation of policy output to satisfy public demand (but paralleled by efforts to secure adequate knowledge), and

1970- : active consultation among policy-makers of different levels to assess "political" feasibility of new policies.

The development of the Canada Water Act is a case in point. As the first major federal response to environmental opinion, and cutting across existing divisions of jurisdictions in water management, this Act functioned as a trial balloon for further federal involvement in environmental policy. Carefully prepared by the bureaucracy, the bill was then subject to negotiations between the national and the provincial governments. The resulting changes were included in the final draft of the bill. During these stages there was also some assessment of the resources of implementation. In performing its usual role of "polishing" the details of the bill, the Parliament also brought in the views of affected interests. The final output contained several changes, mostly introduced by the bureaucracy, accepted by the Cabinet, and ratified by Parliament (Van Loon and Whittington, 1971: 486 ff.).

The proclamation of the Act was upheld for several months because of the discussions of the responsibilities in environmental policy-making which formed a large part of the two Constitutional Conferences held in 1970. The second Conference resulted in a provincial recognition of the need for federal leadership in international and inter-provincial matters and in environmental research and development activities. The Federal Government should also provide financial assistance to the provinces (Dwivedi, 1972-1973: 142 ff.). But with the fundamental constitutional issues unsolved, the two levels of government were supercognizant of the need for continuous policy consultation and program coordination. Three strategies seem to have evolved: (1) federal initiative in areas of clear federal jurisdiction, (2) cooperation in areas of divided jurisdiction, and (3) federal initiative in areas of divided jurisdiction where cooperative efforts fail (Muntz, 1972: 112). The first strategy can be seen in the surprisingly tough federal move to establish "environmental sovereignty" over waters up to 100 miles off shore through the Arctic Waters Pollution Prevention Act. The second strategy was employed in the making of the Clean Air Act. The strength of the "negotiative" atmosphere is shown in the fact that the third strategy has not had to be employed as yet. The structures through which these federal-provincial policy negotiations take place include among others (1) Constitutional Conferences and Prime Minister meetings, and (2) the meetings of the environmental Ministers in the Canadian Council of Resource and Environmental Ministers, which was established in 1962. This Council has no legislative powers but has provided a useful structure for environmental policy negotiations (De Laet, 1972: 11 ff.).

The Artic Waters Pollution Act seems to be the only major exception from the incrementalism typical of the policy development after 1969. With respect to the question of new policy-making groups or coalitions, one can point to the Special Committee on Environment, set up by the Parliament. But with the limited impact of the Canadian Parliament on policy-making, the Committee's influence is probably felt mostly in details, not in principles, of the policies. Like Sweden, Canada has established an Environmental Advisory Council. But also like Sweden, Canada has chosen not to give this Council any status independent of the Cabinet or the environmental bureaucracy. With much of the environmental research organized inside the Department of the Environment, it is likely that the accumulation of adequate knowledge will increase the bureaucracy's role. This is all the more true since many of the scientist-dominated environmental groups of 1969-1970 are said to have lost much of their vigor and workers in 1972 (Dwivedi, 1972-1973: 151 f.; Muntz, 1972: 120 f.). On the other hand, the possibilities of federal-provincial conflict may provide a check on the national bureaucracy which is not present in the Swedish situation.

The American system of government seems to reflect a deliberate effort to strike a balance between unity and diversity. The unity of the system requires for its vigor and viability abroad a competitive diversity of institutions, processes and participants. The sprawling multitude of this balance-of-powers system—with so many policy-making centers and with its curious coalition of interest and personality rather than party politics—is evidently also present in the overall picture of environmental policy-making at the federal level. This would seem to prevent any attempt to generalize about the American development, or at least make such an attempt both difficult and hazardous. Despite this, some overall patterns will be discussed.

As in Sweden, it seems possible to identify three stages in American environmental policy-making, each with its own characteristics:

pre- 1965: investigation and problem definition;

1965-1969: growing efforts toward a national environmental policy and specific action programs; and

1969- : policy escalation and policy conflict, with both incremental and spectacular changes.

The policy-making before 1965 was fragmented, with different policies for different aspects of the man-environment relationship. However, this period seems to display the following characteristics:

(1) a limited number of participants in the process;

(2) incremental bargaining and compromise: "majority-building," and

(3) emphasis on research and technology development.

There was no consistent White House commitment to the existing policies. Established agencies seemed to differ in power. The agencies concerned with "traditional" conservation programs, such as forestry and national parks, were generally more powerful and visible in the policy-making process than those concerned with "new" programs of pollution control. The process was dominated by a rather small number of Congressmen, who were skillful in the art of bargaining with interest groups and administrative agencies, and in building Congressional majorities for new programs. The moderate importance of environment as a focus for public policy is also shown by the fact that there was no significant jurisdictional dispute between Congressional Committees; rather, jurisdiction over environment as an emergent issue was established as a function of a Congressman's interest in the matter of concern (Cleaveland et al., 1969: 72 ff., 24 ff.; Sundquist, 1968: 323 ff.).

The situation after 1965 changed with respect to the number of participants in the policy process, while the other two characteristics remained. President Johnson's message on "Natural Beauty" signalled a White House commitment to at least some aspects of the environmental problem, and was the first White House effort to set an agenda for environmental policy-making in Congress under the rubric of "the new conservation." Special Task Forces helped set Presidential priorities, and administrative agencies presented draft legislation (Sundquist, 1968: 361 ff.). But even if the President seemed to take the initiative in such areas as nature conservancy and highway beautification, the Congress kept its strong position in pollution matters. And with the President increasingly absorbed in the foreign policy and civil rights issues, the Congress again became the focal point (Caldwell, 1971: 181). With the emerging opinion and media coverage of environmental matters, a certain competition between Congressmen and Committees seemed to appear. Two approaches can be identified: (1) a drive towards a national environmental policy founded on a comprehensive ecological perspective, and (2) an emphasis on the strengthening of existing programs. There even seemed to appear a jurisdictional dispute between these two approaches as farsighted politicians tried to establish themselves in the field. But in both cases, there was a conscious attempt to secure adequate knowledge before action was taken, and compromise and majority-building were still prevalent (Jones, 1972).

The situation under the Nixon Administration seems to have upset some of the earlier characteristics. The increases in public opinion, and the constant monitoring of environmental policy-making by the media, have contributed to what I referred to above as policy escalation and conflict, displaying the following characteristics:

(1) expansion of the number of participants in policy development;
(2) active competition among politicians to be credited with strong legislation; and
(3) a tendency to develop policies without regard to knowledge basis or feasibility.

The first and second developments can be viewed from three aspects. In the Executive, the expansion has had two dimensions. First, the implementation of NEPA established such bodies as the Council on Environmental Quality (CEQ), and dissatisfaction with progress toward pollution control led to the establishment of the Environmental Protection Agency (EPA) (Caldwell, 1971: 226 ff.). But it is typical of the Nixonian drive to concentrate political power to the Executive Office that he has created such a body as the National Industrial Pollution Control Council (NIPCC), which is said (Steck, 1972: 28 ff.) to have reviewed EPA's proposals for guidelines even before these guidelines were made available to the public for comments, and that there has been a considerable expansion of the policy role of the Office of Management and Budget in the environmental field (Rathlesberger, 1972: 266 ff.).

In the Congress, the passage of the National Environmental Policy Act in 1969 was surprisingly smooth, although the Act is probably the most far-reaching environmental legislation on the books. And in 1970, there seemed to be no need for majority-building, but rather a need for a policy to the existing majority (Jones, 1972). Throughout the last years, there has been a buildup of the conflict between different Committees over environmental jurisdiction, and a sharpening of the competition between the "Jackson" comprehensive approach and the "Muskie" approach of strong program legislation. Among the Interest Groups, there have emerged a number of environmental lobbyists, some of which have at times been quite influential in policy development. For at least in the early 1970s, the industrial lobbyists lost some of their "knowledge monopoly" in this field to the environmental lobbyists, and turned increasingly to the Executive with their demands, where they had a channel through NIPCC.

With repect to the tendency to develop policies without regard to appropriate knowledge or implementation feasibility, at least three examples come to mind; (1) the National Environmental Policy Act of 1969, (2) the Clean Air Act Amendments of 1970, and (3) the Water Pollution Control Act Amendments of 1972. In addition to the formulation of national environmental policy goals, the Congressionally sponsored NEPA contains action-forcing provisions for grand changes in administrative behavior (Caldwell, 1971: 192). The development after 1970 suggests that NEPA really represents a break and that the administrative feasibility of its provisions had not been assessed (Council on Environmental Quality, 1971: 25 f., 163 ff. and 1972: 221 ff.). The 1970 Amendments of the Clean Air Act have been described by Jones (1972: 9) as "speculative augmentation" and policy "beyond capability." The deadlines for emission-free cars by 1975-1976 were not set because of evidence of technical feasibility, but to protect public health. That a Congressional majority was willing to sponsor such gambling with knowledge is said to have been caused by the dramatic upsurge in public opinion in 1970 (Jones, 1972). The third example, the 1972 Amendments of the Water Pollution Control Act, set 1985 as the deadline for the achievement of "no discharge" of pollutants into American waters. The Senate Public Works Committee reported that "pollution continues because of technological limits," implying that the goal of "no discharge by 1985" would stimulate an increase in technological development and thus lift off existing limits (United States Senate Public Work Committee, 1971: 8, 12). Exactly why the Congressional majority went along with this escalation of policy is not clear to me at this point. However, the fact that the Amendments were passed only a few weeks before the Presidential election, and the fact that the authorizations of the Amendments were fervently challenged by Nixon, seem to have contributed to the Congressional behavior. It is thus conceivable that the environmental policy will become part of the conflict over Congressional-Presidential power during Nixon's second term.

I will summarize these preliminary findings by discussing environmental policy-making in terms of policy characteristics—styles of policy-making and use of knowledge—in relation to the findings. Theoretically, policy-making could range from *incrementalism*—small, consecutive moves and changes brought about by already existing majorities. Usually, but not necessarily, incrementalism is accompanied by an adaptive use of knowledge. Augmentation might be accompanied by a conjectural approach to knowledge; politicians hope that technical knowledge will somehow solve the problems in implementing policy goals. As I noted above, environmental policy is characterized by highly scientific-technological knowledge needs and costly, far-reaching effects. At the same time, it is characterized by an increase in public demand for political action. But as the preliminary findings show, these characteristics are not strong enough to impose a common policy-making pattern in all three countries.

Even if the figure shows that the style of environmental policy-making has been predominantly incremental and adaptive, this does not mean that environmental policy characteristics are the causal factor. Rather, it is a

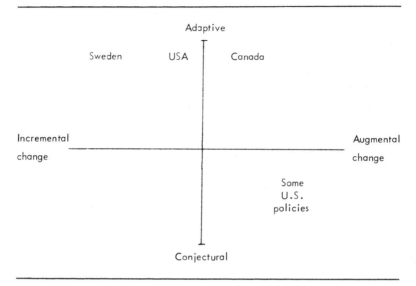

Figure 2: Patterns of Environmental Policy-Making in Canada, Sweden, and the United States: Use of Knowledge, Type of Change.

reflection of existing styles, be it the "compromise-culture" of Sweden, the necessary majority-building in the personality politics of the United States, or the constitutional negotiations of Canada. It is plausible that the break from this predominant style should occur in the United States with its competitive policy-making centers and its personality politics, probably rendering it more susceptible to dramatic shifts in reactions to public demand than the disciplined party systems of Canada and Sweden.

WITHIN THE OUTPUT

AREA AND CONTENT OF ENVIRONMENTAL POLICIES

In this section an attempt will be made to present an overview of the scope and character of environmental policies in the three countries. Given the socio-economic and technological similarities between these countries, and the similarities in public pressure for governmental action, one would presume that the scope of the policy area would be about the same for all the countries. A closer look reveals that for certain parts of the policy area, political factors of a structural and/or ideological character are important factors in the determination of governmental involvement.

The "core" areas of environmental policy (nature conservancy, environmental R & D, pollution control) are thus covered in all three countries. The fact that Sweden has not discussed weather modification and control in terms of environmental policy could probably be referred to calculations of utility. Relatively smaller than Canada and the United States, Sweden may find such efforts less important but also impossible without international cooperation. Albeit there is a Solid Waste Management Branch within Environment Canada, this area is still seen as a big problem facing the federal government, with answers yet to be found (Morley, 1972a: 18). If it were to propose national legislation in this field, the national government would have to move very carefully, because of the provincial jurisdiction over land and matters of a local character. In the area of environmental education, differences can be found in the relative weight given to specific parts of governmental action. Sweden has stressed information and propaganda to the public (National Environmental Protection Board, 1972: 188 f.), while Canada has been accused of withholding information (Dwivedi, 1972-1973: 152). In 1973, the Nixon administration announced that it regards the Environmental Education Act of 1970 as a legitimate target for efforts to cut Federal spending by discontinuing appropriations for the programs of environmental education within the Department of Health, Education, and Welfare (Office of Management and Budget, 1973: 433 f.).

TABLE 1
ENVIRONMENTAL POLICY AREA:
CANADA, SWEDEN, AND THE UNITED STATES

Category	Canada	Sweden	USA
Environmental Education (education, information, propaganda)	X	X	(?)
Environment R & D	X	X	X
Hazardous Products Control (environmental contaminants, poisonous or toxic products)	(?)	X	(?)
Land Use Planning	(?)	X	(?)
Nature Conservancy (national parks, nature and wilderness reserves, outdoor recreation)	X	X	X
Pollution Control (air, marine, noise, soil, water, radiation)	X	X	X
Solid Waste Management	(?)	X	X
Water Resources Management	X	X	X
Weather Control and Modification	X	—	X
Wildlife Management	X	X	X

X = categories covered by governmental action at national level
(?) = governmental action ambivalent or not yet taken
— = not recognized as within policy

The most interesting differences occur when one looks at such areas in which private use of natural resources and private economic activity become involved and subject to environmental regulation. With respect to hazardous products control, the long-standing view of environmentalists has been that the producer should be required to prove his product is harmless before he is allowed to use it. This calls for some substantive involvement in business activities, and is bound to meet some ideological objections. While the governmental actions all seem to be very alike in content, they differ in timing. Mostly, the actions taken or proposed call for governmental authority to acquire information—either through governmental testing or through information from producers—of the potential dangers of their products, and for control of production, importation, handling and utilization of such products. Such an act was passed in Sweden in the spring of 1973 (Lundqvist, 1973c). In Canada, there have been sections in certain laws bearing on this subject, but no national legislation or policy. A new Environment Contaminants Act will, however, be presented to the Parliament sometime in 1973 (Governor-General of Canada, 1973). In the United States, the 92nd Congress (United States Senate Committee on Interior and Insular Affairs, 1973: 677 f.) did not pass Presidential legislation on the matter, but Nixon has again proposed such policies to the 93rd Congress (National Archives and Records Service, 1973: 147). The differences in timing and in the ease with which action has proceeded seem to be due to traditional views towards the relationship between governments and business, although I am not quite sure of this assertion at this point. The kind of cooperative and compromising atmosphere existing between the Swedish government and industrial interest no doubt made the new regulations easier to muddle through than did the United States system, where powerful industrial interests take a more adversary view of governmental regulations.

In most modern political systems, land-use planning has been considered primarily a matter of local jurisdiction. However, the increasing concern for the environment has lead to the recognition that many land-use decisions have ramifications of a national character. Efforts have therefore been made to develop policies which would make possible both various economic uses and ecologically wise management of natural resources, at the same time trying to avoid changes in existing jurisdictional arrangements. Clearly, divided jurisdictional powers in a federal system may provide a formidable hindrance to the formulation and legitimization of a national land-use policy.

In Canada, the provincial jurisdiction over land use and matters of a local character, combined of course with an ideological bias toward private property rights, all seem to have contributed to the fact that at the national level, the Land Inventory Branch of Environment Canada is occupied mostly with the acquisition and production of data on land capabilities (McCormack, 1971; Environment Canada, 1972a: 16). To establish a land-use policy, the federal government must negotiate with the provinces or else declare the matter to be of urgent national concern.

In the United States, several land-use policy proposals were discussed during the 92nd Congress. A Land-Use Policy Act was indeed passed in the Senate, but never reached the floor of the House. Several amendments adopted by the Senate show that the same factors as those in Canada have been at work. To save the rights of the state in land-use planning, amendments were passed which took away federal sanctions against states not meeting the deadlines set out in the Act (United States Committee on Interior and Insular Affairs, 1973: 164 ff.). However, it seems safe to predict that a land-use policy will come out of the 93rd Congress.

Several factors seem to have contributed to the relatively easy incorporation of land-use planning into the Swedish environmental policy. As a unitary state, Sweden faces no jurisdictional hindrances. There are also certain already existing intrusions into private property, such as the traditional right to common access to land, and the regulations of coastal zone properties. Probably the long standing acceptance of central planning also helped in the relatively easy adoption of the resource-management and land-use legislation of 1972 (Lundqvist, 1972b).

Governmental action can take on several forms: regulation of conflicts and behavior; extraction of resources from society; distribution of such resources to members of society; and finally, organization of polity and society for successful conduct of the other types of action. Of course, most policies contain combinations of all these contents. The assertion was made above that these forms are known to all political systems, but that differences in patterns of legitimacy, tradition, power, and utility may result in policy differences between countries. Some existing policy typologies (Salisbury and Heinz, 1970: 47 ff.) ascribe a strong influence on policy content to such factors as the amount of (1) integration in the demand for political action, (2) integration in the decision-making system, and (3) costs of gathering adequate predecision information. It should already be clear that all these factors play an important part in determining the content of environmental policies. There are, however, certain characteristics of environmental problems that deserve attention here; (a) their character of "public" goods, with (b) a frequently "non-tangible" character of the benefits to be expected, which all leads to (c) a "non-constituency" character of many environmental policy issues, since outputs concern "everybody." Thus, even with an increasingly integrated—or strong—public demand, it is not very probable that truly "self-regulative" or truly "distributive" policies will be the original choice in this policy field.

According to some existing theories about policy content (Salisbury and Heinz, 1970), the factors just mentioned work towards some structural or "organizational" policy. A cursory look at the three countries suggests some commonalities. They have all established central environmental administrations which in each country cover approximately the same field of authority. There are, however, certain organizational differences. In Canada, most administrative Services concerned with environmental problems are parts of the new Department of the Environment. Thus most policy functions, from overall policy planning to detailed implementation, are contained within the same organizational unit. On the other hand, both Sweden and the United States have different organizations for the "political" and "administrative" components of environmental policy. In Sweden, the overall political responsibility for environmental policy rests with the Department of Agriculture, while the administrative functions are carried out by the National Environment Protection Board. This arrangement reflects the Swedish tradition of establishing independent agencies for policy implementation. In the United States, the policy functions formally rest with the Council on Environmental Quality, an advisory body within the Executive Office of the President, while the administrative ones are carried out mostly by the Environmental Protection Agency. It should be mentioned, however, that while Environment Canada and the Swedish NEPB both cover some of the traditional conservation policies, the EPA has no authority on such matters. With regard to the difference between policy and administrative functions, it should be noted that both the Swedish and United States agencies seem to be expanding their role in policy matters. Finally, the large federal countries Canada and USA have struggled to establish some organizational entities on an interregional or "problem-shed" basis, while small, unitary Sweden has made no moves in such a direction.

In the choice between regulation and some sort of distributive arrangement as alternative of environmental policy implementation, the governments seem to follow a temporal sequence. Being the original choice, the "regulative" mode is still dominant. From air pollution control to wildlife management, the three countries rely heavily on regulation of individual, corporate, and collective behavior as the prime means of goal achievement. But although this regulation in all the countries extends from standard setting and quality control enforcement to outright management of environmental services, some interesting differences should be mentioned. In unitary Sweden, the power to regulate behavior for the nation as a whole rests with the Parliament, which means that regulatory environmental policies have an immediate nationwide applicability. But in the United States—despite the tendency towards Federal preemption of this policy field—regulatory pollution policies usually provide for a time limit within which the states are supposed to make the regulations they deem necessary or appropriate to meet Federal environmental quality criteria. Not until such time limits have elapsed without state action, or the Federal authorities find state efforts inappropriate, can Federal regulation take over. And even if the Federal government in Canada can decide on, e.g., national ambient air quality criteria, direct regulation of pollution sources is under the jurisdiction of the Provinces.

In connection with this discussion of "regulative—self-regulative" policies, the United States NEPA of 1969 deserves special attention, since it differs from other legislation in the environmental field. Aside from setting broad national environmental policy goals, NEPA contains several action-forcing provisions of a "quasi" self-regulative character. All agencies are required to "develop and use" procedures, methods and approaches which will ensure that environmental values enter decision-making processes along with economic and technological considerations. NEPA also contains the specific requirement to include, in any decision "significantly affecting" the human environment, a detailed statement of the environmental impact of the proposed action. To the architects of NEPA, these provisions are a means whereby agencies and officials would be forced to reorient their policies, planning and procedures in order to put into effect the environmental policy objectives specified in preceding sections of the Act (Caldwell, 1973). As it turns out, however, this "quasi" self-regulative character of NEPA has not yielded generalizable results. The agencies have been reluctant to change their behavior in the directions indicated by the Act. Many of the changes have instead had to be initiated through court action (Council on Environmental Quality, 1972: 248 f.; United States Senate Committee on Interior and Insular Affairs, 1973: 1025). Nevertheless, NEPA has had a measurable effect on departmental planning and decision-making, particularly in view of the risk involved in failure to comply with the terms of the Act if challenged in court.

Earlier, I pointed to environmental quality as having the character of a "collective good." The difficulty in distributing environmental quality per se does not, however, imply that "distributive" policy elements have not been used, nor does it preclude the introduction of "extractive" components in environmental policies. If one looks at these two types of policy contents as the positive and negative ends on a continuum of governmental economic incentives to certain economic and political entities for actions which preserve and restore environmental quality, one can find at least three characteristics. First, such policy components are used in varying fashions in all three countries. Second, "traditional" distributive techniques such as subsidies and grants are most common. Third, there seems to be a tendency to mix positive and negative economic incentives in what has been called a "self-executory" approach. This new approach seeks to minimize governmental regulation by combining charges, fees, and other extractive devices with positive incentives in an effort to cause polluters to adopt environmental protection measures in their own economic self-interest and with a minimum of costs.

All three countries use these policy components towards both local communities and private industries. But while differences in their use towards local communities seem to reflect only differences in views of technical feasibility, the variations found with regard to their use towards industries seem to reflect differences on principles. In Canada, Federal support to municipal sewage treatment is given in the form of loans, with 25 percent of the loan "forgivable" if the plant is finished within the planned time (Habitat, 1970: 72 f.). The Swedish grants are tied to the degree of purification reached by the plant (National Environmental Protection Board, 1972: 111). On the other hand, the United States federal grants are based on the "needs" of the states as determined by a state by state analysis of planned treatment facilities in each states (United States Senate Committee of Interior and Insular Affairs, 1973: 570). While all three countries have adopted rapid depreciation allowances for pollution control equipment as a legitimate subsidy to industries, only U.S.A. and Canada have introduced tax credits and tax exemptions. The United States tax credits are the same as for all other industrial investments, and the tax exemptions are for industrial revenue bonds. In Canada, the federal sales tax is eliminated for pollution control equipment. In the field of direct subsidies, it might be somewhat surprising to find that the allegedly "socialist" government of Sweden is the only government among the three to give direct subsidies for pollution equipment installations, regardless of the size of the company. The subsidies are for old plants, however, and will not be given after 1974 (Royal Ministry for Foreign Affairs et al., 1972: 56). Under the 1972 Amendments of the United States water pollution control legislation, so called "small" businesses can get direct subsidies, but only if certain specified conditions have been met (United States Senate Committee on Interior and Insular

Affairs, 1973: 575). The Canadian view has been that "the polluter must pay," but it has also been implied that the whole array of distributive and extractive policy instruments with regard to pollution control will be reconsidered for the period beginning 1974 (Muntz, 1972: 93; House of Commons, 1970: 4746).

For years, economists have argued that the present combination of regulative standards and distributive means is a very inefficient way of reaching environmental policy goals. Instead they argue for some kind of a "self-executory" approach. By putting charges and fees on the use of the environment, be it for extraction of natural resources or for disposal of wastes, the total costs of using the environment would have to be taken into consideration, and the users would thus get an incentive to change the utilization of the environment in such a way that they can evade the costs of charges or fees. There is clear evidence that this approach to environmental policy content is receiving more and more attention and is gaining in importance. The Canada Water Act of 1970 contains several provisions for effluent discharge fees in designated water quality management areas (Morley, 1972: 13 f.). The Swedish Royal Commission on Environmental Costs is supposed to present some recommendations on charges and fees in early 1974 (Lundqvist, 1973c). In his 1973 environmental message (National Archives and Records Service, 1973: 146 f.), President Nixon came out strongly in favor of this self-executory approach, and for the third time proposed charges on the emission of sulfur oxides. Several bills in the 92nd Congress display this growing interest in charges and fees as an important element of environmental policy (United States Senate Committee on Interior and Insular Affairs, 1973: 896 ff.).

Thus, all countries reveal a trend towards a "charges and fees" approach, which indeed could be viewed as a "self-regulative" one. From existing theories of policy content, it can be deduced that increases in integrated demand and in costs of acquiring appropriate predecision information, work toward the adoption of such policies, especially if the decision costs in the form of majority-building also are high. It is tempting to speculate that, since demand integration has been increasing, and since the costs of acquiring appropriate information on environmental relationships, causes and effects are increasing accordingly as new research results are published, this approach will indeed be more attractive to dispersed federal systems than to integrated unitary ones.

FROM OUTPUT TO OUTCOME

IMPLEMENTATION AND ENFORCEMENT OF
AIR QUALITY PROGRAMS

How do our "potentially influential" factors and the characteristics of environmental problems affect policy implementation? To reach some tentative conclusions on this problem, I will discuss four issues:

(1) basic approaches and methods of implementation;
(2) division of authority between levels of government;
(3) methods of assuring compliance and their use; and finally,
(4) provisions with regard to participation in the implementation process.

The discussion will be confined to the area of air quality programs, which may to some extent jeopardize the possibility of generalizations on environmental policies as a whole. To be sure, air pollution problems can vary between regions and countries depending on the types of pollutants, climate, etc. On the other hand, the consequences of air pollution—to health, to property, and to aesthetics—are roughly the same everywhere. Further, air quality programs share the qualities of other environmental programs; they deal with a truly "collective" good, and they are heavily based on science and technology. Finally, the "cosmopolitan" character of air pollution leads one to assume that certain implementation techniques are diffusable all over the world.

Before proceeding further, some technical points should be clarified. Air pollution stems from either stationary or mobile sources. The former type can be controlled chiefly by two methods or combinations of them. The "Air Resource Management" (ARM) approach means that standards are set for the concentration of pollutants in *ambient* air. The "Best Available Technology" (BAT) sets standards for maximum levels of air pollutants emitted from specific sources with a view to the latest developments in abatement technology. Pollution from mobile sources may be attacked in a number of ways, ranging from regulation of the composition of fuels to incentives for changes in transportation policies. The discussion here will be mostly confined to programs concerning pollution from stationary sources.

There is thus considerable variation between the three countries. In Canada, the constitutional situation plays an important role. There is a direct provincial responsibility to control air pollution, and the provinces

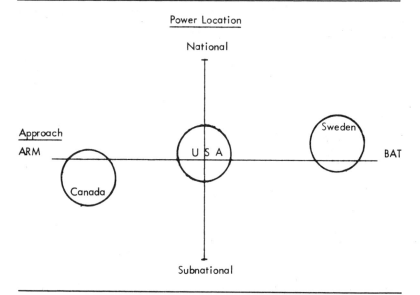

Figure 3: Air Pollution Control Programs (Stationary Sources) in Canada, Sweden, and the United States: Basic Approach and Location of Program and Police Powers.

can exercise both program and policy powers. Thus, although the Clean Air Act of 1971 purports to promote a uniform approach and to give the Federal level a leadership role, it can only supplement provincial action. The Federal government can act unilaterally only if the pollution comes from Federal works, if it is hazardous to human health or if it leads to violation of international agreements of which Canada is part. In all other cases, the Federal government must engage in negotiations and agreements with Provinces. Both constitutional realities and political necessities make the Federal choice restricted to the ARM approach if it wants to act unilaterally to abate air pollution. By this approach, the Federal government can take credit for an active rule without violating the rights of the Provinces (Lucas, 1971: 11, 16; Morley, 1972b: 16 ff.).

Originally, the United States approach was that of ARM. The "air shed" concept in the 1967 Air Quality Act meant that the country was to be divided into "atmospheric areas" and "air quality regions" on the basis of meteorological, topographical, and urban-industrial factors. The Federal authorities were to establish criteria for main pollutants, containing information as to their health effects and to the costs of preventing such pollution. The states were then to use their power to set ambient air quality standards and their policy powers to formulate and implement plans for the pollutants for which criteria had been established. Only in certain specified cases could the police powers be referred to the Federal level (United States Senate Committee on Interior and Insular Affairs, 1971: 62 ff.).

This pattern was drastically changed with the "augmental" Clean Air Act Amendments of 1970. There is now a *combination* of ARM and BAT approaches plus a considerable expansion of the program and police powers at the Federal level. All areas not otherwise designated are now considered as air quality control regions, and air quality criteria for remaining major pollutants have been established. The ARM approach at the Federal level was strengthened in that procedures were established for setting *national* ambient air quality standards; primary ones to protect public health, secondary ones to protect public welfare. Following the promulgation of these standards, the States develop plans for implementing the primary standards. The introduction of the BAT approach is seen in the new powers for EPA to formulate emission standards for (a) pollutants hazardous to human health, and (b) new emission sources. The States have the power to formulate standards for existing emission sources. The 1970 Amendments considerably increased the policy powers of the Federal level by giving the Administrator of the EPA several mandatory functions with regard to enforcement of control programs (Council on Environmental Quality, 1971: 8 ff., 1972: 111 ff.; Rathlesberger, 1972: 13).

The basic Swedish approach to stationary sources of air pollution has been one of BAT. The Environment Protection Act of 1969 contains the principle that everyone intending to engage in polluting activities must take such protective measures as can be "reasonably demanded" with a view to what is technically and economically feasible. There is no explicit mention in the Act of air quality regions, ambient air quality standards, or references to public health. Several specified types of industries must either obtain a permit from the Franchise Board for Environment Protection, or a so called "permit exemption" from the National Environment Protection Board. In both cases, the conditions under which polluting industrial activities can be carried on are determined, as well as the protective measures to be taken by the applicant. To determine the requirements of "technical and economic feasibility," source emission standards were promulgated early in 1970 for those industries mentioned in the Act. Police powers to see that the conditions set out in permits or exemptions are adhered to are shared between the central NEPB and the

25 State Regional Boards, with the NEPB as the coordinating body (Royal Ministry for Foreign Affairs et al., 1972). It is officially intended that this BAT approach will be combined with an ARM approach in 1974. Ambient air standards are already set for sulfur dioxides, and other ambient air standards are considered for introduction and promulgation (Emmelin, 1973).

The Canadian situation seems to be one of consensual style and limited public participation. In setting national air quality objectives, the Federal Minister of the Environment has a statutorily recognized discretion to seek the advice of, and to consult with, industry, labour, provincial and municipal authorities, and any other person interested in the matter. But although Environment Canada has stated that "it is our policy to seek comments and suggestions from all interested parties before final promulgation of regulations" (Lucas, 1971: 16), the process through which the 1971 objectives for five major pollutants were established does not indicate a wide interpretation of the authority. The agreement with the provinces was based on a recommendation "by a committee of Federal and Provincial experts after an examination of the scientific data" describing the effects of the five pollutants on various receptors (Lucas, 1971: 11). And although the Federal Minister has coercive powers to

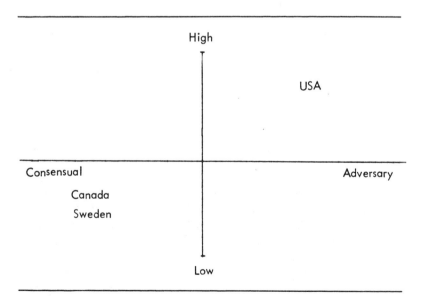

Figure 4: Air Pollution Control Programs (Stationary Sources) in Canada, Sweden, and the United States: "Styles" of Implementation and Enforcement, Degree of Participation.

obtain information from polluters, such information is mainly obtained without the use of sanctions. The precedent of consensual cooperation with water polluting industries in setting effluent discharge standards (Environment Canada, 1972b: 42) seems likely to determine the strategy also in the field of air pollution control. The confinement to mostly expert participation in policy implementation is said to be typical of Canadian system as a whole.

The process through which source emission standards were established in Sweden reveals a great deal about the consensual style of policy implementation in that country. In order to find out the technological and economic bases for the standards, joint branch committee were set up with representatives from the regulated industries and from NEPB. While the former studied the technological and economic aspects of abating air pollution, the latter mostly confined themselves to obtaining data on foreign standards. On the basis of the reports and recommendations of these committees, and with commentaries solicited only from the participating industrial branches, standards were promulgated early in 1970. Many of the promulgated standards show signs of earlier industrial proposals. As mentioned earlier, industries which want to continue with their polluting activities must either obtain a permit from the Franchise Board or a "permit exemption" from the NEPB. The court-like procedures of the Franchise Board also include public hearings in the local community of the applying industry, and several other sections of the Environment Protection Act contain provisions for public participation. However, the regulated interests prefer—by a ratio of 6 to 1—to apply for "exemptions." Through this "exemption" procedure, the conditions for continued industrial activity are settled in "negotiations" between the NEPB's "exemption unit" and the industries concerned, with much less stringent rules for public participation in the process (Lundqvist, 1971: 174 ff.).

In contrast, the American situation seems to be characterized by a much larger degree of participation and by a more adversary implementation style. Both of these features reflect the strong position of judicial action in the American system. The 1970 Amendments prohibit violation of any implementation plan, emission standard or other provision. They provide criminal penalties and give several mandatory functions to the EPA Administrator. In addition, the Act authorizes citizen suits against polluters to enforce compliance with standards and suits against the EPA Administrator if he fails to implement his mandatory functions. The Act provides for public hearings and permits judicial review of standards, plans and other actions taken under the Act. The evidence so far suggests that most of these provisions have been used.

The EPA established primary and secondary standards in 1971, then published draft versions of its guidelines for state implementation plans, and invited public comments. Subsequently, the EPA has—in addition to approval of some plans—given extensions to some states to meet the deadlines of implementation. These decisions—like the EPA's omission of "anti-degradation" clauses in its guidelines—have been challenged in court by both industrial and environmental interests. Industrial interests have also challenged the EPA's standards for new emission sources, saying that the EPA failed to comply with the impact statement clause of NEPA and thereby closed off participation in the standard-setting process. Another sign of openness was the hearings held on standards for hazardous pollutants. The EPA has also invoked its emergency powers to shut down polluting industries (the Birmingham episode of November 1971, Environmental Protection Agency, 1972: 1 ff., 92 f.). However, the openness of the process has been challenged by House Subcommittee findings that OMB and NIPCC have in fact had final influence on state plan promulgation (United States Senate Committee on Interior and Insular Affairs, 1973: 625 ff.).

It seems clear that these differences can be related to four potentially influential factors. Constitutional realities, ideological beliefs and traditional ways of making decisions all seem to have worked against direct source regulation in the United States and Canada. At the same time, environmental interest groups were emerging as politically important factors, and some positive action had to be taken. The adoption of the ARM approach clearly reflects these circumstances, and it also reflects the long standing of public health as a legitimate Federal concern. The changing approach in the United States in 1970 reflects the dramatic upsurge in the power of environmental interests in that country. In Sweden, on the other hand, regulation of industry has a long record, and thus no legitimacy concerns or traditions worked against the adoption of the BAT approach. However, the strong power of industrial interests in policy implementation is reflected in the formulation of the Swedish emission standards. Utility calculations probably also played a part in the choice of approaches. The small size of Sweden does not seem to warrant a system of air sheds and air quality regions like the one developed in the United States. To what extent scientific knowledge played a part can only be subject to speculation at this point. Since the ARM approach is based on the criterion of air pollution effects on public health, one could hypothesize that such an approach warrants more scientific research resources than the BAT approach, and that it could therefore be more easily adopted in a large country where such resources exist. The need for

Sweden to take part in OECD research before adopting the ARM, as well as the similarity of the Canadian "acceptable" to the United States "secondary" ambient standards, seems to give some credit to such a conclusion.

ALL THE WAY AROUND–
ENVIRONMENTAL POLICIES AND CHANGE

The discussion so far has focussed on environmental policies as dependent variables. The findings indicate that the characteristics of environmental policies—which could be thought of as universal and working toward commonalities in environmental policies—have not been strong enough to offset the influence of system-specific features. The differences found in environmental policy processes and contents seem to vary with differences in the factors identified as potentially influential. Under such circumstances one might be led to believe that the study of environmental policies as independent variables and changing forces in politics would not be a worthwhile effort. It should be remembered, however, that if seen as coherent bodies of governmental action, they have been part of politics for only a short time. Therefore, their impact might not yet be fully felt, although there are almost daily indications of their ramifying tendency. As far as the more direct impact on environmental quality is concerned, there is still a lot of dispute among scientists, technicians, and politicans over the proper ways to measure such impact. The discussion here will be focussed on the more indirect impact on politics and political change—as such change was defined above—without in any way implying that this kind of impact can be more easily measured than the former one. Out of necessity, the discussion will be as much conjectural as empirical.

As a changing force, a lot of the success of environmental policy will depend on how much it penetrates and sets premises for other policy areas. On purpose, the earlier discussion of policy area did not adopt a dynamic perspective. However, a most striking development in this field is the expansion of the policy-relevant area. In such policy areas as transportation, energy, agriculture, urban planning and regional development, environmental considerations form new constraints on policy action. Water-borne transportation of oil is becoming more and more restricted by environmental concern, as can be seen in Canada's laws regarding Arctic waters. Pollution control laws are restraining energy policies, which is perhaps most clearly seen in the United States. There, the impact statement process of NEPA has caused several delays in the development of nuclear power plants, and it has held up the construction of the Alaskan oil pipeline. Bans on pesticides are setting new premises for agriculture and forestry. Air and noise pollution controls are altering the basis of urban planning. In Sweden, land-use planning has developed out of environmental concerns and is setting new premises for industrial expansion and regional development. Many of these changes are the result of one important aspect of environmental policy, i.e., the fundings for environmental research. So far, the expansion seems to have had the following impact on political change:

(1) *Change in structures:* new environmental bureaucracies; new "ecological" administrative units.

(2) *Change in performance levels:* increased legislative and administrative output.

(3) *Change in power relations:* legislatures-administrations-(courts): central-regional; among interest groups.

The establishment of new national environmental bureaucracies has already been discussed under "organizational" policy. These administrative units are still expanding. The United States, and to some extent Canadian, adoption of structural innovations of an "ecological" character—air and water quality control regions—has also been mentioned. And although differences have been found in administrative approaches and styles of implementation, the overall pattern is one of increased bureaucratic output. Standards, regulations, and control programs have been promulgated at a sometimes surprising rate. And while the increase in legislative output cannot be said to be a result of policy impact alone, it is true that much of the increase is due to earlier allocation of resources to environmental research and investigations. The budget figures of the early 1970s show some considerable increases in all the three countries.

It is when one looks at changes in power relations that differences in policy impact can be found. The tip of the balance to environmental bureaucracy is most clearly felt in Sweden, and also in Canada, although the constitutional situation in that country may provide a checking point. The reason for this development is mainly the immense concentration of knowledge to the bureaucracy, which is a consequence of closeness to the problems of implementation, but also of the control over environmental research. Despite the establishment of the EPA, the United States Congress still has a comparatively strong influence over environmental policy. The special position of the Congress in a balance-of-powers system and the informative role of Congressional staff and investigatory units, plus the means of public hearings, seem to make the Congress less vulnerable to bureaucratic "usurpation" than its Canadian and Swedish counterparts. Thus the United States Congress seems to be the only legislature where environmentalist groups find it worthwhile to lobby for their cause. Apart from the "power of the purse," several aspects of environmental policy work in a centralizing direction, e.g., the central promulgation of state implementation plans in the United States, which shifts power to the Federal level.

In Sweden, the impact has been one of centralization in an already very centralized system. A case in point is the national physical planning, which puts new environmental restraints on the local communities in their planning and development activities. While the Canadian constitution may be a check on centralizing tendencies, the Federal power to set environmental standards for Federal works, fisheries, shipping and navigation, combined with the control over spending and research, may gradually lead to an increase in centralization. Environmental policies have had an impact on power relations insofar as they put restrictions on public agencies and private firms and invoke judicial powers through the intervention of environmental groups. The outstanding example is the United States, where the NEPA and the air and water pollution legislations open up a number of possibilities for environmentalists to influence the behavior of agencies and firms through actions in court. This has lead to a rather conspicuous increase in the importance of courts in United States environmental policy (Council on Environmental Quality, 1972: 278 ff.). No such dramatic impacts can be seen in the other two countries.

Finally, a few words on a policy impact that is more susceptible to conjectural speculation than to empirical assertion, i.e., the impact on cultural values. We have seen that environmental opinion increased rather conspicuously in the years up to 1970. The question is whether the input of public demand has changed in amount or character during the years of policy implementation and, if so, what the reasons are for such changes. With regard to the amount of public demand, there has been much talk about a backlash in the last years. While not many polls are available, at least one taken in the United States (American Institute of Public Opinion, 1972) indicates that there is still a considerable majority in favor of pollution control policies even if they mean increased spending. It has still to be proven that the increasing ramifications—in individual comforts, in consumer costs, in jobs, etc.—of environmental policy are cutting off public support for the case. However, some instances of conflict between "labor" and "ecology" have occurred in Sweden. They are probably one reason why the Swedish government is trying to combine the "outdoor" environmental policy with efforts to clean up the working-place environment. In the United States, the United Automobile Workers have tended to side with the auto manufacturers where environment measures threatened jobs.

One reason for this talk about a decrease in environmental demand is probably the change in the character of these demands. One impact of ongoing policy implementation is that the demands have to become more sophisticated as the implementation goes on. Certainly, concepts like "ambient" or "emission air standards" do not lend themselves to mass movement causes as easily as "crisis" or "scandal." This need for sophistication is reflected in the "bureaucratization" of environmental groups, most easily seen in the Swedish and United States systems. In the United States, a handful of environmentalists were speaking on behalf of the environmental movement during several crucial policy events in 1972 (National Journal, 1972: 1025-1034). This, however, still leaves us with the Canadian case, where the spokesmen of the environmental movement seem to have quit in considerable numbers in the last year. One is led to ask whether environmental policies are successful to such an extent that people leave the field because their demands have been satisfied. This, however, does not seem to be the case. Two consecutive polls in Canada show that a considerable segment of the public is either doubtful or undecided in their view of the adequacy or success of governmental environmental policies (Canadian Institute of Public Opinion, 1972 and 1973).

CONCLUDING REMARKS

Since most of this paper is in itself a summary, I will not make another one here. Instead, I will discuss some problems which seem to arise out of this study, problems which are linked both to political science and—in a wider sense—to politics in general. The most intriguing one seems to be that of the relationships between public demand, policy process, and governmental action. The problem could be viewed in terms of what has been called "models of governing" (Rose, 1973b). The discussion on policy impact seems to indicate that there occurs a shift in models of governing during the policy process. While the "liberal" model—in which public demands lead to governmental action—seems to be the dominant in the beginning of a policy, the model of "court politics"—in which political and bureaucratic leaders handle policy problems without much public involvement—seems to be a more accurate description of the later stages of the policy process. It may also be that ongoing policies are characterized by this model of governing. Much more research along the lines of policy dynamics must be done to find out whether this is a general developmental pattern (Peters, 1972).

This still leaves us with the problem of "anticipation." This is neither a reaction to existing demands, nor is it action isolated from movements in public opinion. But is it just another way of "liberal" governments to pursue the path of conflict avoidance by trying to settle a compromise for the direction and scope of future actions? Maybe a possible hypothesis for further comparative policy research is that there is in fact evolving a new model of governing in the form of a fusion of "liberal" and "court" politics. The development of a so-called "technocracy" seems to imply a need for governing processes whereby drastic shifts in public opinion are anticipated and avoided and the vested interests of the technocracy are left unchanged. Comparative policy studies should be carried out with a view to the implications of such new techniques as opinion polls, computer simulations, and long-term planning for this hypothetical fusion of models of governing.

REFERENCES

American Institute of Public Opinion (1972) Gallup Opinion Index, Report No. 87 (September): 12. Princeton, N.J.: AIPO.

ANTON, T. J. (1960) "Policy-making and political culture in Sweden." Scandinavian Political Studies 4: 82-102.

CALDWELL, L. K. (1973) "The National Environmental Policy Act: status and accomplishments." Proceedings of the Thirty-Eighth North American Wildlife and Natural Resources Conference held at Washington Hilton Hotel March 18-21. Washington, D.C.: Wildlife Management Institute (forthcoming).

––– (1971) Environment: A Challenge to Modern Society. Garden City: Doubleday.

Canadian Institute of Public Opinion (1973) The Gallup Report released March 7. Toronto: CIPO.

––– (1972) The Gallup Report released June 24. Toronto: CIPO.

––– (1970a) The Gallup Report released March 25. Toronto: CIPO.

––– (1970b) The Gallup Report released December 2. Toronto: CIPO.

CLEAVELAND, F. N. and associates (1969) Congress and Urban Problems. Washington, D.C.: Brookings Institution.

Council on Environmental Quality (1972) Environmental Quality. The Third Annual Report of the Council on Environmental Quality. Washington, D.C.: Government Printing Office.

––– (1971) Environmental Quality. The Second Annual Report of the Council on Environmental Quality. Washington, D.C.: Government Printing Office.

DE LAET, C. (1972) "Development of environmental policies in a federal state." Invited paper for the session on national and international environmental policies, IUCN 12th Technical Meeting at Banff, Canada, September 11-16 (mimeo).

DOERN, G. B. and P. AUCOIN [eds.] (1971) The Structures of Policy-Making in Canada. Toronto: Macmillan of Canada.

DWIVEDI, O. P. (1972-1973) "The Canadian government response to environmental concerns." International Journal (Toronto) 28 (Winter): 134-152.

EMMELIN, L. (1973) "Sulfurous pollution: the Air Quality Criteria approach." AMBIO 2 (February-April): 12.

Environment Canada (1972a) Annual Report 1971-1972. Ottawa: Information Canada.

——— (1972b) Canada and the Human Environment. A contribution by the Government of Canada to the United Nations Conference on the Human Environment, Stockholm, Sweden, June 1972. Ottawa: Information Canada.

Environmental Protection Agency (1972) A Progress Report. December 1970-June 1972. Washington, D.C.: Government Printing Office.

ERSKINE, H. (1972) "The polls: pollution and its costs." Public Opinion Quarterly 36 (Spring): 120-135.

Governor-General of Canada (1973) The Speech of the Throne, First Session, Twenty-Ninth Parliament. (January 4) Ottawa: The Queen's Printer.

Habitat (Ottawa) (1970) "Sewage treatment across Canada: federal loans and forgiveness." Volume 13, 5/6: 72-74.

HANCOCK, M. D. (1972) Sweden: The Politics of Postindustrial Change. Hinsdale, Ill.: Dryden Press.

House of Commons (1970) Debates (March 12): 4746-4747. Ottawa: The Queen's Printer.

JONES, C. O. (1972) "Characteristics of environmental politics: the case of air pollution." Paper prepared for delivery at the 1972 Annual Meeting of the American Political Science Association, Washington Hilton Hotel, Washington, D.C., September 5-9 (mimeo).

LUCAS, K. C. (1971) "The federal role in air pollution control in Canada." Ottawa: Air Pollution Control Directorate/Department of the Environment. (Document APCD 71/19.)

LUNDQVIST, L. J. (1973a) "The comparative study of environmental policy." Policy Studies Journal 1 (Spring): 138-143.

——— (1973b) "Crisis, change and public policy. Considerations for a comparative study of environmental policy." European Journal of Political Research 1 (Spring).

——— (1973c) "Environmental policy and administration in a unitary state: Sweden," in L. K. Caldwell (ed.) Organization and Administration of Environmental Programmes. With special reference to the recommendations of the United Nations Conferences on the Human Environment, Stockholm 5-16 June 1972. New York: United Nations Department of Economic and Social Affairs, (forthcoming).

——— (1972a) "Sweden's environmental policy." AMBIO 1 (June): 90-101.

——— (1972b) "Sweden's national physical planning for resources management." Environmental Affairs 2 (Winter): 487-504.

——— (1971) Miljövårdsförvaltning och politisk struktur. Lund: Prisma/ Verdandidebatt.

McCORMACK, R. J. (1971) "The Canada land-use inventory: a basis for land-use planning." Journal of Soil and Water Conservation 26 (July-August): 141-146.

McEVOY III, J. (1972) "The American concern with environment," pp. 214-237 in

W. J. Burch, Jr., N. H. Cheek, Jr., and L. Taylor (eds.) Social Behavior, Natural Resources and the Environment. New York: Harper & Row.

MORLEY, C. G. (1972a) "Federal environmental legislation: a survey." Paper delivered to the Chemical Institute of Canada Seminar, Quebec City, June 7 (mimeo).

——— (1972b) "A cooperative approach to pollution problems in Canada." Paper delivered to the Society of Engineering Science First International Meeting, Tel Aviv, June 12-17 (mimeo).

MUNTZ, G. H. (1972) "Federal government policy and the issue of inland water pollution." M. A. Thesis. Guelph: Univ. of Guelph.

National Archives and Records Service (1973) Weekly Compilation of Presidential Documents 9 (February 15): 144-153. Washington D.C.: Government Printing Office.

National Environment Protection Board (Stockholm) (1972) Statens naturvårdsverk Årsbok 1971. Stockholm: Allmänna förlaget.

National Journal (1972) "Exemptions from NEPA requirements sought for nuclear plants, pollution permits." Volume 4 (June 17): 1025-1034.

Office of Management and Budget (1973) The Budget of the United States Government Fiscal Year 1974: Appendix. Washington, D. C.: Government Printing Office.

PETERS, G. B. (1972) "Public policy, socio-economic conditions, & the political system." Polity 5 (Winter): 277-284.

RATHLESBERGER, J. [ed.] (1972) Nixon and the Environment. The Politics of Devastation. New York: Village Voice/Taurus Communications.

ROSE, R. (1973a) "Concepts for comparison." Policy Studies Journal 1 (Spring): 122-127.

——— (1973b) "Models of governing." Comparative Politics 5 (July).

——— (1972) "Why comparative policy studies?" Policy Studies Journal 1 (Autumn): 14-17.

Royal Ministry for Foreign Affairs, Royal Ministry of Agriculture (1971) Sweden's National Report to the United Nations on the Human Environment. Stockholm: Norstedt & Söner.

Royal Ministry for Foreign Affairs, Royal Ministry of Agriculture, National Environment Protection Board (1972) Environment Protection Act, Marine Dumping Prohibition Act. With Commentaries. Information to the United Nations Conference on the Human Environment. Stockholm: Norstedt & Söner.

SALISBURY, R. and J. HEINZ (1970) "A theory of policy analysis and some preliminary applications," pp. 39-60 in I. Sharkansky (ed.) Policy Analysis in Political Science. Chicago: Markham.

SKARKANSKY, I. (1970) 'The political scientist and policy analysis," pp. 1-18 in I. Sharkansky (ed.) Policy Analysis in Political Science Chicago: Markham.

SIMEON, R. (1971) Federal-Provincial Diplomacy. The making of recent policy in Canada. Toronto: Univ. of Toronto Press.

STECK, H. J. (1972) "Power and the policy process: advisory committees in the federal government." Paper delivered at the 1972 Annual Meeting of the American Political Science Association, Washington Hilton Hotel, September 5-9 (mimeo).

SUNDQUIST, J. L. (1968) Politics and Policy: The Eisenhower, Kennedy, and Johnson Years. Washington, D.C.: The Brookings Institution.

U.S. Senate Committee on Interior and Insular Affairs (1973) Congress and the Nation's Environment. Environmental Affairs and Natural Resources affairs of the 92nd Congress. Prepared by the Environmental Policy Division, Congressional Research Service, Library of Congress at the request of Henry M. Jackson, Chairman, Committee on Interior and Insular Affairs, United States Senate. Washington, D.C.: Government Printing Office.

——— (1971) Congress and the Nation's Environment. Environmental Affairs of the 91st Congress. Prepared by the Environmental Policy Division, Congressional Research Service, Library of Congress at the request of Henry M. Jackson, Chairman, Committee on Interior and Insular Affairs, United States Senate. Washington, D.C.: Government Printing Office.

VAN LOON, R. J. and M. S. WHITTINGTON (1971) The Canadian Political System: Environment, Structure, & Process. Toronto and Montreal: McGraw-Hill of Canada.

LENNART J. LUNDQVIST is currently Research Assistant of the Department of Political Science of the University of Uppsala, Sweden. He served for one year (1972-1973) as Visiting Assistant Professor of the Department of Political Science and the School of Public and Environmental Affairs at Indiana University. He received his B.Soc.Sc. and his Ph.D. from the University of Uppsala. He is author of Miljövårds-förvaltning och politisk struktur *(Lund: Prisma 1971) and several articles in professional journals. His field of interests includes comparative and environmental public policy and administration.*

183917